# STARS OF HIP-HOP

# JAY-Z

## HITMAKER AND BUSINESS LEADER

EILEEN LUCAS

**Enslow Publishing**
101 W. 23rd Street
Suite 240
New York, NY 10011
USA
enslow.com

Published in 2020 by Enslow Publishing, LLC.
101 W. 23rd Street, Suite 240, New York, NY 10011

**Library of Congress Cataloging-in-Publication Data**
Names: Lucas, Eileen, author.
Title: Jay-Z : hitmaker and business leader / Eileen Lucas.
Description: New York : Enslow Publishing, 2020. | Series: Stars of hip-hop |
Audience: 2 | Includes bibliographical references and index.
Identifiers: LCCN 2018048703| ISBN 9781978509580 (library bound) | ISBN
9781978510166 (pbk.) | ISBN 9781978510180 (6 pack)
Subjects: LCSH: Jay-Z, 1969—Juvenile literature. | Rap musicians—United States—
Biography—Juvenile literature.
Classification: LCC ML3930.J38 L84 2020 | DDC 782.421649092 [B] —dc23
LC record available at https://lccn.loc.gov/2018048703

Printed in the United States of America

**To Our Readers:** We have done our best to make sure all websites in this book were active and appropriate when we went to press. However, the author and the publisher have no control over and assume no liability for the material available on those websites or on any websites they may link to. Any comments or suggestions can be sent by email to customerservice@enslow.com.

**Photo Credits:** Cover, p. 1 Kevin Mazur/Getty Images; pp. 5, 17 Johnny Nunez/ WireImage/Getty Images; p. 7 Jamie McCarthy/WireImage/Getty Images; p. 8 Al Pereira/Michael Ochs Archives/Getty Images; pp. 11, 14 Sylvain Gaboury/FilmMagic/ Getty Images; p. 13 Chris Walter/WireImage/Getty Images; p. 18 © AP Images; p. 20 Scott Gries/Getty Images; p. 23 James Devaney/WireImage/Getty Images; p. 24 Theo Wargo/Getty Images; p. 26 John Ricard/Getty Images.

# CONTENTS

# COMING FROM NOTHING

The bike was too big for Shawn. A four-year-old was on a two-wheeled bike! Shawn rode it anyway. The neighbors were amazed. Shawn called it a taste of being famous. "I liked it," he said. "Felt good."[1]

Shawn Corey Carter was born December 4, 1968. He became the famous rapper and successful businessman Jay-Z. But he started out poor in Brooklyn. His family lived in the Marcy **Projects**. This is where the poorest people lived.

Jay-Z attends the premiere of the video game *NBA 2K13* in 2012. He produced the game and hosted the party at his 40/40 Club in New York City.

## A GIFTED CHILD

Shawn's dad was Adnis Reeves. He left when Shawn was young. His mom, Gloria Carter, worked hard. She did her best to care for Shawn, his sisters, and his brother.

Shawn was a good student. He loved to read. He also liked to think up rhymes.

## The Marcy Projects

Jay-Z grew up in a "project." Projects are crowded apartment buildings. They were built for poor people who couldn't afford to live anywhere else. There was a lot of crime there. Jay-Z rapped about this in his songs.

He wrote them down on scraps of paper. Then he'd stuff them in his pocket. He also wrote rhymes in a notebook. Sometimes he woke the family up at night. He was tapping out a beat for his rhymes.

## SURVIVING THE STREET LIFE

Shawn's mom worked a lot. He started spending time on the streets. He began selling drugs. Shawn saw what drugs, especially **crack**, did to people. Drugs

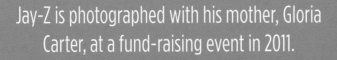

Jay-Z is photographed with his mother, Gloria Carter, at a fund-raising event in 2011.

destroyed lives. He didn't use drugs. But selling them became his job.

Selling drugs put Shawn's life in danger. Guns and knives were everywhere. He was

Jay-Z (*right*) was in his early twenties in this photo with hip-hop artists Jaz-O (*left*) and Queen Latifah.

afraid of being beaten or killed. He worried about going to jail.

Shawn met a rapper named Jaz-O. Maybe rap could lead to a better life. Jay-Z became Shawn's rap name.

"All I got is dreams, nobody else can see. Nobody else believes, nobody else but me."[2]

## RAPPING ON THE SPOT

Jay-Z kept writing rhymes. He rapped at parties. Jay-Z rapped every chance he could. He often rapped "**freestyle**." This means he could make up rhymes on the spot. He said what "someone who comes from nothing" had to say.[3]

# FIVE YEARS, FIVE ALBUMS

**D**amon Dash was a businessman from East Harlem. Harlem is part of New York City. Dash and Jay-Z both loved hip-hop. In 1995, they started a company together. They called it Roc-A-Fella Records. Dash ran the business side of it. Jay-Z took care of the music part.

In 1996, they recorded Jay-Z's first album. It was called *Reasonable Doubt*. Jay-Z rapped about life on the streets. He said it was telling "the truth of our lives."[1]

Jay-Z celebrates Damon Dash's birthday at
a party for his partner in 2002.

## ONE OF THE RAP GREATS

Another rapper's voice is on Jay-Z's first
album. His name was the Notorious B.I.G.
Sometimes he was just called Biggie. Jay-Z
and Biggie became friends.

Jay-Z was working on his second album,
*In My Lifetime, Vol. 1*. He learned some
bad news. Biggie had been shot and

## Meaningful Rhymes

For Jay-Z, rap was part reporting, part having fun, and part art. He created phrases with layers of meaning. He wrote songs about growing up in a world that felt like a war zone.

killed in Los Angeles. There was **conflict** between rappers from the East Coast and those from the West Coast. Still, Jay-Z's new album sold well. Roc-A-Fella got some help from Def Jam Records. Def Jam was big in the hip-hop world.

Jay-Z's next album was one of his most successful. It was called *Vol.2... Hard Knock Life*. Jay-Z won a Grammy Award for it. *Rolling Stone* magazine named Jay-Z the Best Hip-Hop Artist of 1998.

The Notorious B.I.G. performs in 1995. He was killed in 1997.

Jay-Z signs autographs at a 2003 event in a Bloomingdale's clothing store. The Rocawear clothing line has become a huge success.

## GOING INTO FASHION

In 1999, Jay-Z released his fourth album. Another album came out the next year. This made five albums in five years. Jay-Z and Damon Dash started a hip-hop clothing line. They called it Rocawear. Jay-Z wore Rocawear clothes onstage.

Then Jay-Z got in big trouble. He was fighting the **bootlegging** of rap music. He argued with a record producer named Lance Rivera.

"I did bad things [in the past] . . . I try not to do bad things anymore."[2]

One night, Jay-Z lost control. He stabbed Rivera in the stomach. Fortunately, Rivera did not die. Jay-Z served **probation** for the attack. He promised himself he would never get in trouble like that again.

# FORGIVING THE PAST

Jay-Z's sixth album, *The **Blueprint***, came out September 11, 2001. That was the day the United States was attacked by terrorists. But in time, *The Blueprint* became successful.

Jay-Z released another album in 2002. It was called *The Blueprint 2: The Gift & the Curse*. One of its songs featured singer Beyoncé Knowles. They were dating. On Jay-Z's next album, *The Black Album*, Gloria Carter's voice can be heard. Jay-Z recorded his mom as she talked in the studio one day.

Jay-Z also opened his first 40/40 Club. More sports bars in other cities would follow. Many athletes and stars spent time there.

Jay-Z and Damon Dash celebrate the opening of the first 40/40 Club in New York City.

## RETIRING FROM RAP

Jay-Z wanted to take a break from making studio albums. He held a concert in Madison Square Garden. He called it a "retirement party." An announcer said, "The one, the only . . . Jay-Z!"[1] At the end,

Jay-Z performed his "retirement" concert in Madison Square Garden in 2003.

a giant jersey with Jay-Z's name on it was lifted to the roof.

But Jay-Z didn't leave hip-hop. In 2004, he became president of Def Jam Records. This was the company Roc-A-Fella Records had worked with. Jay-Z was president of Def Jam for the next four years.

## NO MORE ANGER

Jay-Z also met up with his dad. Reeves was very ill. "Me and my pop got to talk," Jay-Z

### Hip-Hop Won't Stop

In 2006, two important museums announced a new exhibit. It would tell about hip-hop. Hip-hop wasn't just music from the streets. It had become a key part of America.

Jay-Z and Nas perform together in October 2005.

said. "I got to tell him everything I wanted to say."[2] It still hurt that his dad had left long ago. But in a song, Jay-Z told his dad that he forgave him. Reeves died in 2003.

In 2005, Jay-Z appeared with a rapper named Nas. The two rappers had insulted each other. But they worked it out. Fans were happy when the two rappers shook hands onstage. Then they sang each other's songs.

In 2007, Jay-Z put out his tenth album, *American Gangster.* It sold well. Later, he left his job as president of Def Jam.

"Rappers took the noise of urban life and turned it into music."[3]

# A LONG WAY FROM MARCY

**4**

**M**any rappers want to use their fame to help others. Jay-Z works with "Get Out the Vote" projects. This is a way for people to let their voices be heard. Many places in the world don't have enough water. In 2006, Jay-Z worked with the United Nations to bring attention to this serious problem.

## A GROWING FAMILY

In April of 2008, Jay-Z married Beyoncé. Only close family and friends were invited to the wedding.

Jay-Z and Beyoncé enjoy a basketball game together while dating in 2005.

Jay-Z and Beyoncé had a baby girl in 2012. They named her Blue Ivy Carter. Her cries were recorded on one of her father's songs. It was called "Glory." It quickly hit the **Billboard charts**.

Jay-Z, Beyoncé, and their daughter, Blue Ivy Carter, attend the NBA All-Star Game in 2017.

In spring of 2013, Jay-Z began Roc Nation Sports, a sports **agency**. In 2015, he started working with Tidal. This is an internet **streaming** company. It puts music online.

In June 2017, Beyoncé and Jay-Z had twins. The Carters named their girl Rumi. Her twin brother was named Sir.

The next year, Jay-Z and Beyoncé released an album together as "the Carters." It is called *Everything Is Love*.

## GIVING BACK TO THE COMMUNITY

In 2003, Jay-Z and his mom founded the Shawn Carter **Foundation**. This

### The Rapper Talks Books with Oprah

Jay-Z loves reading. He has named some books that are important to him. He talked about this with fellow book lover and talk show host Oprah Winfrey. She may not like rap, but she respects the rapper.

helps students go to college. In 2005, he promised to give a million dollars to help people after Hurricane Katrina. He has performed with stars such as Bono, the lead singer of U2. They have worked together to support many good causes.

Jay-Z's albums have sold more than fifty million copies. He has received many

Jay-Z and Sean "Diddy" Combs came together to raise money for charity in 2005.

awards. He's had fourteen number one Billboard albums. He is a successful businessman. He loves his family. He has come a long way from the Marcy Projects.

"Every human being has genius-level talent. . . . You just have to find what it is that you are great at, and then tap into it."[1]

# TIMELINE

**1968**  Shawn Corey Carter is born on December 4 in New York City.

**1995**  Jay-Z, Damon Dash, and a third partner form Roc-A-Fella Records.

**1996**  Jay-Z's first album, *Reasonable Doubt,* is recorded.

**2000**  Jay-Z and Damon Dash open the Rocawear clothing company.

**2003**  Jay-Z opens his first 40/40 Club in New York City. Jay-Z holds a "retirement party" concert on November 25 in Madison Square Garden, in New York.

**2004**  Jay-Z becomes president of Def Jam Records, an office he holds for four years.

**2008**  Jay-Z marries Beyoncé Knowles on April 4.

**2012**  Blue Ivy Carter is born on January 7.

**2013**  Jay-Z becomes a sports agent through his company Roc Nation Sports.

**2017**  Twins, Rumi and Sir Carter, are born on June 13.

**2018**  The Carters kick off a tour in the United Kingdom and release a joint studio album called *Everything Is Love.*

# CHAPTER NOTES

## CHAPTER 1. COMING FROM NOTHING

**1.** Jake Brown, *Jay-Z and the Roc-A-Fella Records Dynasty* (Phoenix, AZ: Amber Books, 2006), p. 6.

**2.** Brown, pp. 32–33.

**3.** Lyrics to "History" by Jay-Z, in *Empire State of Mind, How Jay-Z Went from Street Corner to Corner Office* by Zack O'Malley Greenburg (New York, NY: Penguin/Portfolio, 2011), p. 205.

## CHAPTER 2. FIVE YEARS, FIVE ALBUMS

**1.** Jay-Z, *Decoded* (New York, NY: Spiegel & Grau, 2011), p. 16.

**2.** Jake Brown, *Jay-Z and the Roc-A-Fella Records Dynasty* (Phoenix, AZ: Amber Books, 2006), p. 155.

## CHAPTER 3. FORGIVING THE PAST

**1.** Zack O'Malley Greenburg, *Empire State of Mind, How Jay-Z Went from Street Corner to Corner Office* (New York, NY: Penguin/Portfolio, 2011), p. 84.

**2.** Greenburg, p. 95.

**3.** Jay-Z, *Decoded* (New York, NY: Spiegel & Grau, 2011), p. 255.

## CHAPTER 4. A LONG WAY FROM MARCY

**1.** Hardwood Highlight, "Jay-Z - Inspirational That Everyone Is a Genius," YouTube, January 2, 2015, https://www.youtube.com/watch?v=ydsmqw_6YQE.

# WORDS TO KNOW

**agency**  A company that represents an athlete or a person in the entertainment industry.

**Billboard chart**  A list published by *Billboard* magazine that shows how popular songs in different categories of music are each week.

**blueprint**  A drawing that shows the plan for how something will be made or built.

**bootlegging**  The sale of something taken or received illegally.

**conflict**  Fighting.

**crack**  An illegal drug.

**foundation**  A group that is created to give money for a good cause.

**freestyle**  A type of rap made up on the spot.

**probation**  A period of time when someone who has committed a crime has to behave and check in with an officer instead of going to jail.

**projects**  Low-rent housing for the poor often built in large cities.

**streaming**  A way to send or receive video or sound files over a computer in a steady flow.

**urban**  Having to do with large cities.

# LEARN MORE

## BOOKS

Hill, Laban Carrick. *When the Beat Was Born: DJ Kool Herc and the Creation of Hip Hop.* New York, NY: Roaring Brook Press, 2018.

Kampff, Joseph. *Jay Z: Rapper and Businessman.* New York, NY: Enslow Publishing, 2016.

Morse, Eric. *What Is Hip-Hop?* Brooklyn, NY: Akashic Books, 2017.

Oswald, Vanessa. *Jay-Z: Building a Hip-hop Empire.* New York, NY: Lucent Press, 2019.

## WEBSITES

**Jay-Z's Life + Times**
*lifeandtimes.com*
Explore Jay-Z's official website, which includes information on music, fashion, sports, and other projects.

**Kidzworld**
*www.kidzworld.com/article/5321-pioneers-of-hip-hop*
Read about how hip-hop and rap got started.

**The Shawn Carter Foundation**
*www.shawncartersf.com*
Find out more about Jay-Z's organization, which helps low-income students attend college.

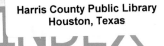
# INDEX

**5**